Contents

CW00956396

How to use this book

Each page has a title telling you what it is about.

Instructions look like this. Always read these carefully before starting.

This shows you how to set out your work. The first question is done for you.

Read these word problems very carefully. Decide how you will work out the answers.

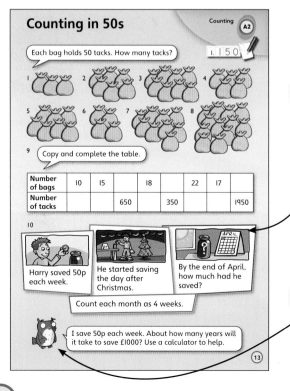

This is Owl. Ask your teacher if you need to do his questions.

Rounding

Round each number to the nearest 10. Use the number line to help.

1. 16 → 20

| | | | | | | | | | | | | | |
|18|19|**20**|21|22|23|24|25|26|27|28|29|**30**|31|

17
16
15

1   16 → ☐   2   23 → ☐   3   46 → ☐

4   43 → ☐   5   37 → ☐   6   51 → ☐

55
54
53

7   34 → ☐   8   22 → ☐   9   48 → ☐

| | | | | | | | | | | | | | |
|52|51|**50**|49|48|47|46|45|44|43|42|41|**40**|39|

32
33
34
35
36
37
38

Now try these.

10. 64 → 60

10   64 → ☐

60 61 62 63 64 65 66 67 68 69 70

11   12 → ☐

10 11 12 13 14 15 16 17 18 19 20

12   73 → ☐

70 71 72 73 74 75 76 77 78 79 80

13   11 → ☐

10 11 12 13 14 15 16 17 18 19 20

14   82 → ☐

80 81 82 83 84 85 86 87 88 89 90

15   74 → ☐

70 71 72 73 74 75 76 77 78 79 80

Choose a multiple of 10 between 0 and 100. Write the numbers which round to your chosen number.

Rounding

Complete each rounding.

1. 42 → 40

1   42 → ☐

40   50

2   86 → ☐

80   90

3   27 → ☐

20   30

4   95 → ☐

90   100

5   12 → ☐

10   20

6   54 → ☐

50   60

Round each price to the nearest 10p.

7. 21p → 20p

7   21p    **8**   42p    **9**   74p    **10**   31p

11   68p   **12**   52p    **13**   57p    **14**   33p

How many numbers between 10 and 50 round down?

Rounding

Round each amount to the nearest 10 asses.

Did you know?

The Romans used coins called asses.

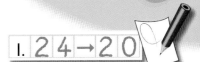

1. 24 → 20

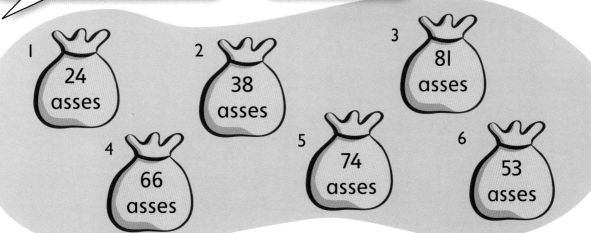

1 24 asses

2 38 asses

3 81 asses

4 66 asses

5 74 asses

6 53 asses

Round each price to the nearest 10 asses.

7. 46 → 50

7 46 asses

8 28 asses

9 31 asses

10 69 asses

11 22 asses

12 53 asses

13 61 asses

14 33 asses

15 38 asses

Think how much each item would cost in pence today. Round to the nearest 10p.

Rounding

Round to the nearest 10.

1. 142 → 140

1 142 → ☐	2 64 → ☐	3 173 → ☐
4 273 → ☐	5 89 → ☐	6 385 → ☐
7 75 → ☐	8 496 → ☐	9 517 → ☐

Round each price to the nearest 10p.

10. £1·34 → £1·30

10  £1·34

11  £2·17

12  £1·21

13  £1·42

14  £1·75

15  £1·82

16  £1·87

17  £1·33

18  £1·58

 Round each amount to the nearest £1. How many amounts between £1 and £2 round down to the nearest 10p?

Comparing numbers

Write the kite numbers in order, smallest first.

1. 4 3 5, 4 4 3

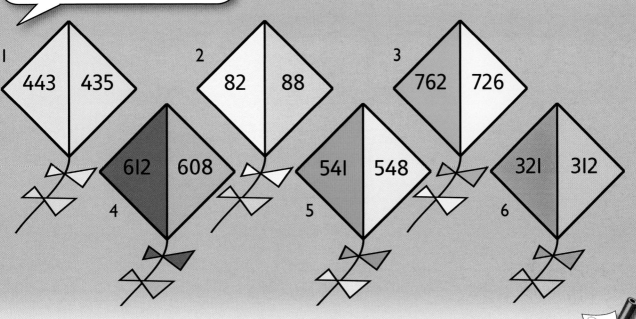

1. 443 435
2. 82 88
3. 762 726
4. 612 608
5. 541 548
6. 321 312

Write a number between the two balloon numbers.

7. 4 7 0

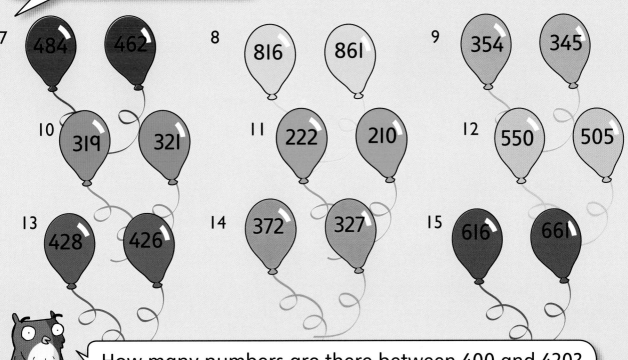

7. 484 462
8. 816 861
9. 354 345
10. 319 321
11. 222 210
12. 550 505
13. 428 426
14. 372 327
15. 616 661

How many numbers are there between 400 and 420?

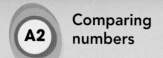

Comparing numbers

Write each pair of dates in order. They are all AD dates.

1. 610, 635

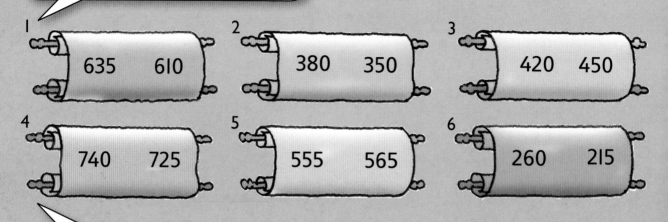

1
635   610

2
380   350

3
420   450

4
740   725

5
555   565

6
260   215

Write a number between each pair of dates.

7
The Romans arrived in AD 43. They left in AD 410. Write a date when the Romans were in Britain.

8
Tom saved £500. Upkar saved £490. Write an amount between the two.

9
One year is 365 days. Two years is 730 days. About how many days are there in $1\frac{1}{2}$ years?

CALENDAR

10
Write two car numbers between these.

365   372

Write your own story comparing two numbers.

Ordering numbers

Put the three numbers in order, smallest first.

1. 365, 370, 381

1 370, 381, 365

2 402, 412, 408

3 550, 524, 502

4 914, 920, 891

5 754, 734, 745

6 969, 696, 966

Add 100 cm to each length.

Write a number between the two lengths.

7. 565 cm, 499 cm

7 465 cm

8 624 cm

9 702 cm

10 299 cm

11 575 cm

12 998 cm

13 650 cm

14 432 cm

I'm thinking of two 3-digit numbers. The digits of each add to 10 and they both end in 0. The difference is 90. What could they be?

Write the two weights in order. Write a weight between the two.

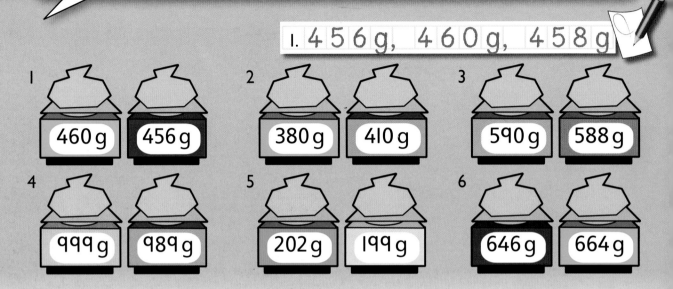

1. 4 5 6 g, 4 6 0 g, 4 5 8 g

1
460 g   456 g

2
380 g   410 g

3
590 g   588 g

4
999 g   989 g

5
202 g   199 g

6
646 g   664 g

7
Use these cards.
Make all the possible 3-digit numbers.
Check you have them all! Now write
them in order from largest to smallest.

4 3 7 8

Write the book prices in
order, smallest first. Write
two prices between.

8. £4·59, £4·99
£4·75, £4·82

8
£4·99   £4·59

9
£6·99   £6·85

10
£9·98   £9·95

11
£4·35   £3·54

12
£2·99   £2·50

13
£3·42   £3·45

Counting in 10s

Write the next three numbers.

1. 70, 80, 90

1 40 50 60

2 10 20 30

3 80 90

4 40 50 60 70

5 120 130 140

6 150 160 170

7 330 340 350

8 560 570 580

9 890 900 910

Each book is 10 cm wide. Count in 10s and write how many books.

10. 5

10
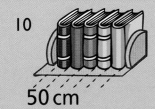
50 cm

11

70 cm

12
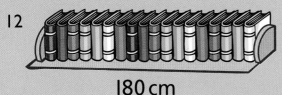
180 cm

13
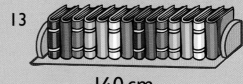
140 cm

14
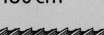
160 cm

15

190 cm

Talk with your partner. If paperbacks are 5 cm wide, how many paperbacks could fit on each shelf?

Counting in 100s

How many times have the children run up and down if they have gone:

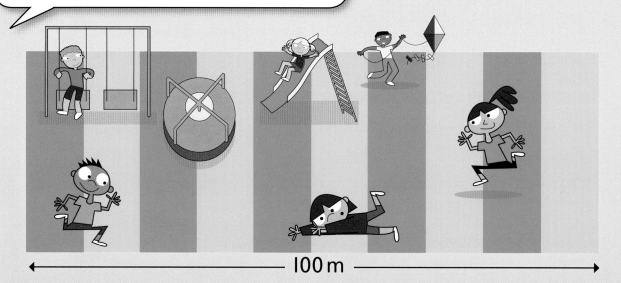

← 100 m →

| 1 | 300 m | 2 | 900 m | 3 | 600 m |
| 4 | 800 m | 5 | 1000 m | 6 | 1200 m |

Each box has 100 pins. How many pins on each tray?

7. 1000 pins

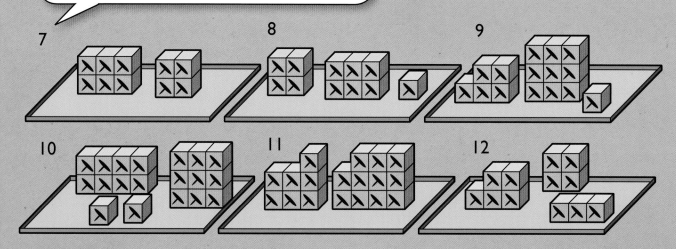

7

8

9

10

11

12

Work out how many boxes are needed to package 1 000 000 pins.

Counting in 50s

Each bag holds 50 tacks. How many tacks?

I. 150 ✓

1

2

3

4

5

6

7

8

9 Copy and complete the table.

Number of bags	10	15		18		22	17	
Number of tacks			650		350			1950

10

Harry saved 50p each week.

He started saving the day after Christmas.

By the end of April, how much had he saved?

Count each month as 4 weeks.

I save 50p each week. About how many years will it take to save £1000? Use a calculator to help.

Counting in 100s and 50s

The bank puts pennies in bags of £1. How many bags? Write the amounts.

1. 8 bags
   67p left
   £8·67

1	867 pence	2	342 pence
3	650 pence	4	900 pence
5	1341 pence	6	1750 pence
7	1840 pence	8	2673 pence
9	1437 pence	10	956 pence

Now imagine that each bag can only contain 50p. How many bags?

11

Felix the cat is too thin!	He eats more and sleeps more.	He gains 50 g each week.	He does this for a year.	How much weight has he gained?

Start counting on from 32. Count in 25s. What is the tenth number? Look at the patterns. Can you predict the 100th number?

Counting in 2s

Write the next four numbers.

1. 12, 14, 16, 18

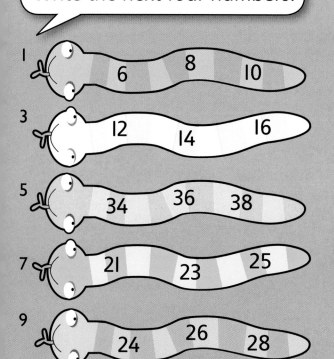

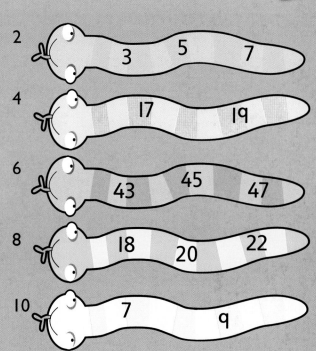

1. 6   8   10
2. 3   5   7
3. 12   14   16
4. 17   19
5. 34   36   38
6. 43   45   47
7. 21   23   25
8. 18   20   22
9. 24   26   28
10. 7   9

Copy and complete the grid. Shade even numbers red. Shade odd numbers blue.

11

1	2	3	4	5	6	7	8	9
10	11	12	13	14	15	16	17	18
19								
	29				33			
37						43		
		48						

Write numbers in a spiral. Colour the even numbers, and look at the pattern.

17	16	15	14	13
18	5	4	3	12
19	6	1	2	11
20	7	8	9	10
21	22	23	24	25

Counting in 2s, even and odd

Count in 2s. Write three numbers forwards and three numbers back.

1. 25, 27, 29, 31, 33, 35, 37

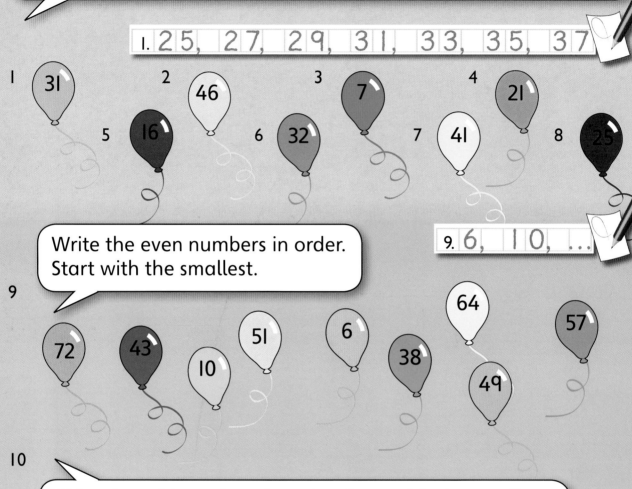

1 31
2 46
3 7
4 21
5 16
6 32
7 41
8 25

9. 6, 10, ...

Write the even numbers in order. Start with the smallest.

9

72 43 10 51 6 38 64 49 57

10 Write the odd numbers in order. Start with the smallest.

Using three odd digits and one even digit, how many 2- and 3-digit even numbers can be made?

11

Work out how many even numbers there are between 250 and 500. How many odd numbers?

Counting in 2s, even and odd

Write each number. Label it even or odd.

1. 8 8 even

 1 88

 2 31

 3 50

 4 64

 5 30

 6 47

 7 53

 8 44

Look at all the numbers. Write double the odd ones. Write half the even ones.

1. 8 8 even
Half = 4 4

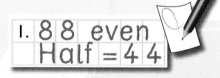

True or false?

9 If you add three even numbers you get an odd number.

10 The difference between two odd numbers is even.

11 Adding 11 to an even number always gives an odd number.

Counting in 2s, even and odd

Write an even number between the two numbers.

1  64 73

2  172 240

3  502 512

4  411 415

5  200 204

6  314 317

7  398 401

8  84 88

Now write an odd number between the two numbers.

Start with a 2-digit number.

9

39 → 40 → 20 → 10 → 5 → 6 → 3 → 4 → 2

2 → 1

If it's odd, add 1. If it's even, halve it.

Keep going like this until you go in a loop!

Try other numbers.

Which ones make long chains? Which make short chains?

I have four cards. Two are even numbers and two are odd numbers. They add to 30. Each card is different. What can the numbers be?

Adding to 10, adding to 100

Write the missing card number to make 10.

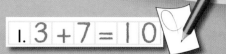
1. $3 + 7 = 10$

1	2	3	4	5	6

 3  2  1  9 8 6

Write the number needed to make 100.

7. $30 + 70 = 100$

7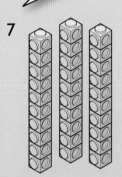

8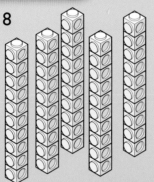

9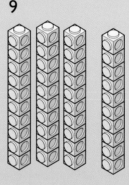

10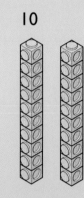

11

12

13

14

Two numbers add to make 100. One ends in a 6. One begins with a 6. What are the numbers?

19

Adding to 100, adding to 1000

Write the number needed to make 1000.

1. $300 + 700 = 1000$

1. 300 ☐

2. 200 ☐

3. 100 ☐

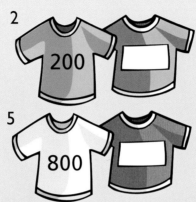

4. 900 ☐

5. 800 ☐

6. 600 ☐

Write the number needed to make 100.

7. $65 + 35 = 100$

7. 65

8. 15

9. 25

10. 55

11. 35

12. 45

13. 75

14. 85

Write some pairs of numbers ending in 5 that add to make 1000.

Adding to 100

Write the change for £1.

1. £1 − 65p = 35p

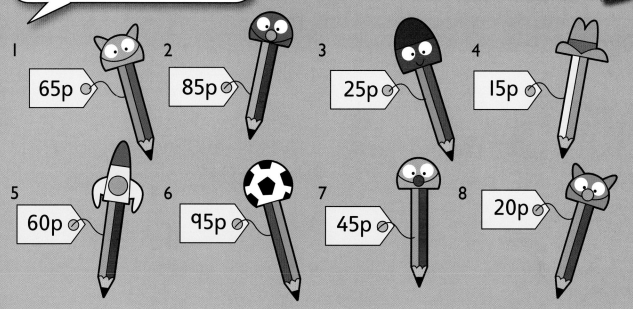

1 65p

2 85p

3 25p

4 15p

5 60p

6 95p

7 45p

8 20p

9 Mon buys a 7p stamp with 10p. He takes his change and adds enough to make £1. How much does he add?

10 Yuko saves £65. Her aunt makes it £100. How much does her aunt add? She spends £45. How much has she left?

11 Old Tom is 100 years old. He spent his life in London and Bristol. If he spent 35 years in London, how long did he live in Bristol?

How many ways are there of making 100 using two numbers ending in 5 or 0?

Adding to £1, adding to next £1

Write the pairs that make £1.

1. $80p + 20p = £1$

1

 55p
 80p
 68p
 45p

 20p
 32p
 60p
 40p

Write the change from £2.

2. $£2 - £1·10 = 90p$

2 £1·10

3 I love fish £1·85

4 £1·60

5 ★ £1·35

6 JOLLY ROGER £1·45

7  £1·15

8 £1·20

9 I LOVE FLOWERS £1·70

 Find ways of making £1 adding three multiples of 5.

Adding to 100, adding to 1000

Write how much longer each tortoise must live to be 100 years old.

1. $60 + 40 = 100$

1
60 years old

2
80 years old

3
70 years old

4
90 years old

5
55 years old

6
40 years old

7
10 years old

8
30 years old

Write the number of years to the year 1000.

9. $700 + 300 = 1000$

9 700

10 600

11 300

12 400

13 800

14 200

15 500

16 900

Your friend writes a 3-digit number ending in 0, e.g. 360. You write a 2-digit number, e.g. 40, to make the next hundred. How many pairs can you find?

Adding to 100, adding to next 100

The wall is 400 cm tall. Write the distance to the top of the wall.

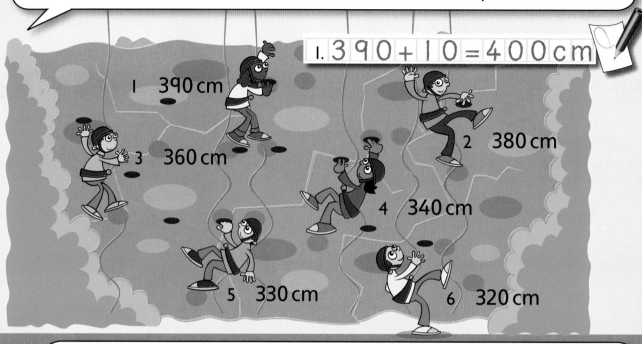

1. $390 + 10 = 400 \text{ cm}$

1   390 cm

3   360 cm

2   380 cm

4   340 cm

5   330 cm

6   320 cm

7   A climber reaches 420 m on a 500 m wall. How far still to climb?

His friend gets halfway up. How many metres has she climbed?

Copy and complete.

8. $480 + 20 = 500$

8    $480 + 20 = $

9    $120 + = 200$

10   $360 + = 400$

11   $270 + 30 = $

12   $460 + = 500$

13   $350 + = 400$

Make up a climbing problem of your own.

Adding to next 100, adding to next £1

The race is 800 m. Write how far to finish the race.

1. $790 + 10 = 800$ m

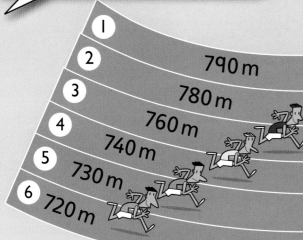

1
2 — 790 m
3 — 780 m
4 — 760 m
5 — 740 m
6 — 730 m
   720 m

FINISH

7

Use these cards. 5 4 6 0 5 0

Create as many ☐☐☐ + ☐☐

where the total is a multiple of 100 as you can.

How much more does each child need?

8. $£3.60 + 40p = £4$

HOCKEY £4·00

SWIMMING £5·00

8 £3·60

9 £3·30

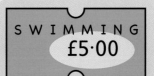

10 £4·80

11 £4·20

Adding to next 100

Copy and complete.

1. $335 + 65 = 400$

1. $335 + \boxed{} = 400$

2. $625 + \boxed{} = 700$

3. $555 + \boxed{} = 600$

4. $465 + \boxed{} = 500$

5. $1300 + \boxed{} = 2000$

6. $815 + \boxed{} = 900$

7. $4800 + \boxed{} = 5000$

8. $1300 + \boxed{} = 1400$

9. $450 + \boxed{} = 1000$

10. $285 + \boxed{} = 300$

11. Jamie saved £3·35. How much must he save to have £4? How much to have £10?

12. Lucy bought a hamster for £8·85. How much change from £10 did she get?

13. Maya had £2·15. Jane had £1·85. How much do they have together? How much more to make £10?

14. Matt has saved £3·85. Steve has saved £4·25. Matt saves 35p a week and Steve saves 25p a week. Who gets to £10 first?

Two numbers add to make a multiple of 100. One is a quarter of the other. What could they be?

Prisms

Are these prisms?

1. Yes

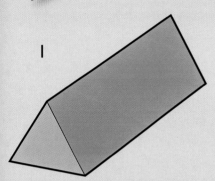 1

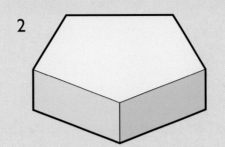 2

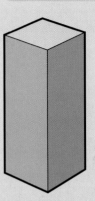 3

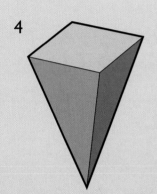 4

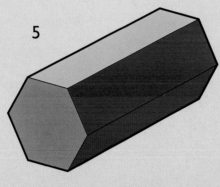 5

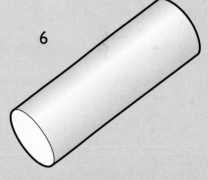 6

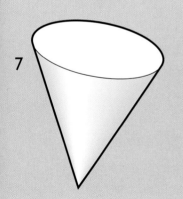 7

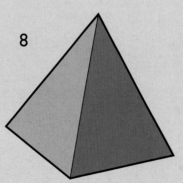 8

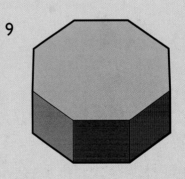 9

Write the names of the end-faces of each prism.

1. Triangles

 Do any prisms roll? Find out.

Describe the faces of each prism.

1. 5 rectangles
   2 pentagons

1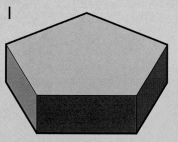

2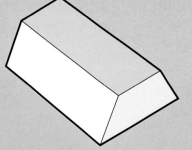

3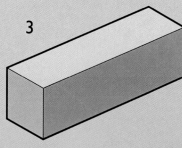

4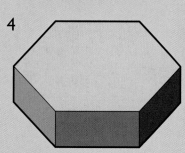

5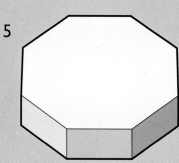

6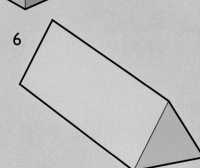

7 Copy and complete this table.

Prism	Faces
Triangular prism	5
Quadrilateral prism	
Pentagonal prism	
Hexagonal prism	
Heptagonal prism	
Octagonal prism	

 I have a prism with 12 faces. What might its end-face look like?

Prisms

Owl thinks that these nets fold to make prisms. Use squared paper and scissors to explore if this is correct.

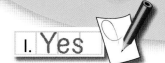

1. Yes

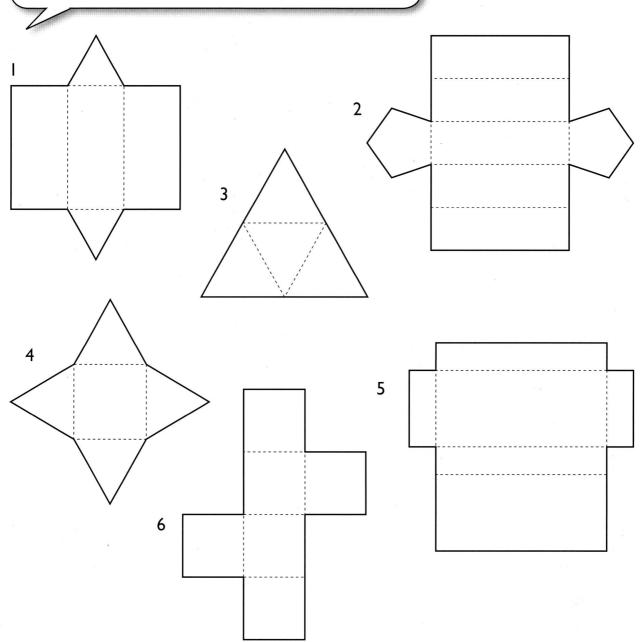

1

2

3

4

5

6

Draw your own net. Give it to your friend to see if it makes a prism. Try your friend's net too.

Flat and curved faces

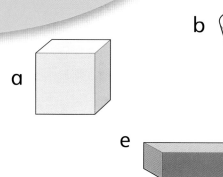

a

b

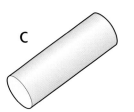

c

d

e

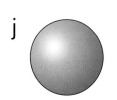

f

g

h

i

j

List the shapes that belong in:

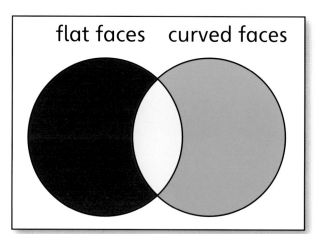

flat faces   curved faces

1 the red section

2 the blue section

3 the yellow section

Which of the shapes have:

4.

4 no flat faces

5 two curved faces

6 no curved faces

7 six flat faces

8 one curved face

9 five flat faces

Invent your own questions about the shapes.

3D shapes

1 Use the words to help you write the name of each shape.

cube   cuboid   cylinder   cone   pyramid   sphere

a
b
c
d
e

f
g
h
i

Write how many:

2 cubes   3 cuboids   4 pyramids   5 cones

6 cylinders   7 prisms   8 spheres

For each shape, write the number of:

9 faces   10 vertices   11 edges

What is the net of a packet of cereal? Draw it.
Explore nets of some of the other packets.

3D shapes

a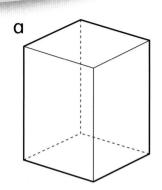

b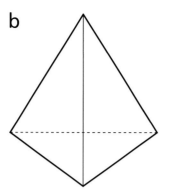

c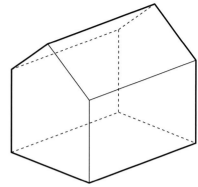

d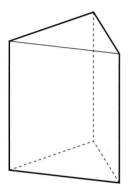

e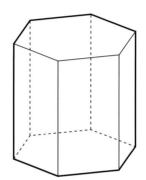

f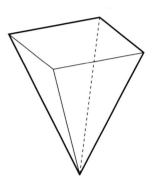

Copy and complete these tables.

shape				a		
faces	4	5	5	6	7	8

shape						
edges	6	8	9	12	15	18

shape						
vertices	4	5	6	8	10	12

Describe the shapes which have an odd number of faces. What other shapes have odd numbers of faces?

3D shapes

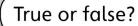

True or false?

1 A cone has a circular face.

2 A cuboid has six vertices.

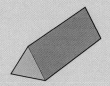

3 A pyramid has triangular faces.

4 A cylinder has no vertices.

5 A cube and a cuboid have equal numbers of edges.

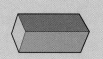

6 A cylinder is a type of prism.

7 All pyramids have the same number of faces.

8 A cuboid only has rectangular faces.

9 Shapes with curved faces only begin with the letter 'c'.

10 A triangular pyramid has the same number of faces as a cube.

11 A pentagonal prism has 15 edges.

Describe the faces of each shape to your partner. Can they guess what it is? Take turns at guessing.

12 square-based pyramid

13 cylinder

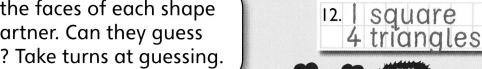

14 triangular prism

15 cube

16 pentagonal pyramid

17 hexagonal prism

Litres and millilitres

Are these 'more than', 'less than' or 'equal to' I litre?

1. less

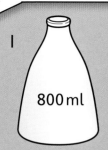
1
800 ml

2
1200 ml

3
1000 ml

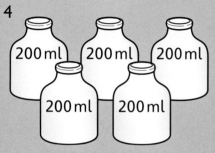
4
200 ml 200 ml 200 ml
200 ml 200 ml

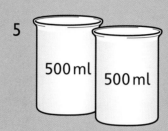
5
500 ml 500 ml

6
250 ml 250 ml 250 ml

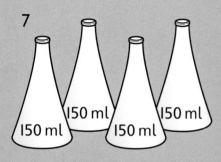
7
150 ml 150 ml 150 ml 150 ml

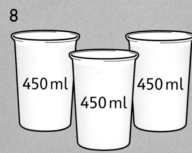
8
450 ml 450 ml 450 ml

9
250 ml 250 ml 250 ml 250 ml

Write how much more or less than I litre each time.

Write the number of millilitres.

10. 1000 ml

10
1 l

11
3 l

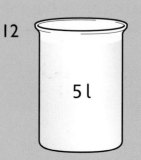
12
5 l

13
$\frac{1}{2}$ l

Litres and millilitres

How much water in each?
Write the answer in millilitres.

I. 800ml

1	2	3	4

5	6	7	8

Write the total amount of liquid in all eight containers.

Write these capacities in litres and millilitres.

9. 1 l 200ml

9	1200 ml	10	2500 ml	11	3100 ml	12	600 ml
13	4000 ml	14	$\frac{1}{2}$ l	15	7200 ml	16	$3\frac{1}{2}$ l

I'm at the supermarket! Which things in my trolley might be measured in litres and millilitres?

Litres and millilitres

Write each capacity in millilitres.

1. 1000 ml

1   1 l

2   1 l 100 ml

3   $1\frac{1}{2}$ l

4   2 l 400 ml

5   5 l 900 ml

6   $3\frac{1}{2}$ l

7   1 l 800 ml

8   $2\frac{1}{2}$ l

9   4 l 700 ml

10 $\frac{1}{2}$ l

11 6 l 300 ml

12 $1\frac{1}{4}$ l

Which of these capacities can be made exactly using a 200 ml cup?

Write the capacities in order, starting with the smallest.

13. $\frac{1}{2}$ l, 800 ml ...

13
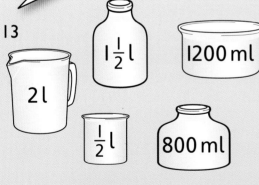

14

15

4 bottles
500 ml each

12 tins
200 ml each

6 cans
250 ml each

Litres and millilitres

True or false?

I. True

1. Half a litre is the same as 500 ml.

2. Five cans, each holding 350 ml, is more than one bottle holding $1\frac{1}{2}$ litres.

3. If I drink 300 ml of orange juice a day, two packs of 1 litre each will last me for a week.

4. Two hundred 5 ml spoonfuls will fill a litre jug.

Solve these problems.

5. A jug holds 250 ml of water. How many jugfuls do I need to fill a sink which holds 6 litres?

6. A recipe needs $1\frac{1}{2}$ litres of chicken stock. A cup of stock holds 15 ml. How many cupfuls of stock are needed for the recipe?

7. A can of fizzy drink holds 300 ml. Gary bought a pack of 12 cans. How much fizzy drink does he have?

8. A tablespoon holds 5 ml. How many tablespoons of medicine are needed to fill a $\frac{1}{2}$ litre bottle?

9. Simret took 250 ml of orange juice to a picnic. She drank half of it at lunchtime, then drank another 65 ml in the afternoon. How much is left in the bottle?

10. A tin of soup holds 450 ml. Bob needs to make enough soup for six people to have 300 ml each. How many tins does he need?

Make up your own story using litres and millilitres.

37

Days and hours

Put each set of letters together to write a day of the week.

1. Friday

1
i a
d F r
y

2
a
u e d y
s
T

3
s n
a
e d W
e d y

4
d a
u n
y
S

5
n M
y d o
a

6
u d
y
S
t a
r
a

7
s
u d
a r
Th y

Write the days in order, starting at Monday.

Write the time these number of hours after midnight.

8. 8 o'clock

8 8 hours

9 10 hours

10 24 hours

11 16 hours

12 21 hours

13 12 hours

14 25 hours

15 40 hours

16 50 hours

I slept from midnight to 6 o'clock. How many hours did I sleep? It was not 6 hours!

Minutes and hours

Write the number of minutes.

1. 6 0 minutes

1 1 hour

2 2 hours

3 1 hour 20 minutes

4 2 hours 10 minutes

5 $1\frac{1}{2}$ hours

6 2 hours 50 minutes

Write the number of hours and minutes for these walks.

7. 1 hour 20 minutes

7 80 minutes

8 60 minutes

9 120 minutes

10 75 minutes

11 30 minutes

12 180 minutes

I fly alongside the walkers. If I fly 1 km every 10 minutes, how far do I get each time?

13

The hockey match has 35 minutes for each half and a 10-minute break at half time. How long does the match last?

14

The train to York takes 2 hours 35 minutes. How many hours and minutes does it take to go to York and back?

Minutes and hours

Write the number of seconds for keeping the football in the air.

1. 60 seconds

1 I minute

2 2 minutes

3 I minute 30 seconds

4 2 minutes 10 seconds

5 I minute 15 seconds

6 $3\frac{1}{2}$ minutes

Write the number of minutes and seconds for skipping.

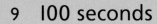
7. I minute 20 seconds

7 80 seconds

8 90 seconds

9 100 seconds

10 120 seconds

11 150 seconds

12 85 seconds

13 72 seconds

14 130 seconds

15 145 seconds

 You are sponsored 5p per skip. Estimate how many skips in I minute. How much will you raise?

16 The first song on my CD plays for 3 minutes I second and the second song plays for 2 minutes 55 seconds. How long does it take to play both songs?

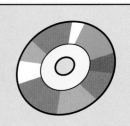

Hours, minutes and seconds

Write how long in hours and minutes.

I. 1 hour 30 minutes

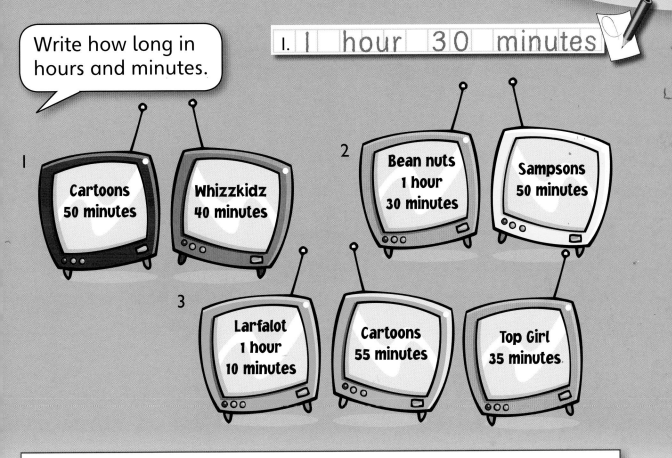

1
Cartoons 50 minutes
Whizzkidz 40 minutes

2
Bean nuts 1 hour 30 minutes
Sampsons 50 minutes

3
Larfalot 1 hour 10 minutes
Cartoons 55 minutes
Top Girl 35 minutes

How many:

4 hours in I week

5 seconds in I day

Think of some questions to ask your friend, e.g. the number of hours in the current month. (You have to know the answer!)

True or false?

6 There are 24 days in I hour.

7 There are more seconds in half a minute than hours in a day.

8 There are 120 minutes in 2 hours.

9 There are more hours in 2 days than minutes in half an hour.

41

Frequency tables

Study the table. Answer the questions.

Favourite snacks	Votes
Crisps	16
Biscuits	7
Rice cakes	2
Bread sticks	10
Cakes	14
Chocolate bars	18
Yoghurt	6
Fruit	4

1 Which is most popular?

2 Which is least popular?

3 Which snack got 14 votes?

4 How many like fruit?

5 How many like yoghurt?

6 How many prefer cakes and chocolate bars?

7 How many like bread sticks and crisps?

True or false?

8 More children like bread sticks than chocolate.

9 More children like cakes than like fruit.

10 Fewer children like yoghurt than like rice cakes.

Draw your own frequency table using votes from your family and friends.

Frequency tables

1 Use the headings and the information to draw and complete your own frequency table.

Favourite pastimes	Votes
Board games	
Cards	
Dominoes	
Quiz games	
Word games	

4 don't like anything but cards.

96 like board games best.

28 like dominoes best.

54 like word games.

57 like quiz games best.

Answer these questions:

2 How many more children like dominoes than like cards?

3 How many children like the two least-favourite pastimes?

4 Which three pastimes are most popular?

5 Which pastimes have less than 50 votes?

Think of five different computer games. Draw your own frequency chart to represent your friends' opinions.

Frequency tables

Study the frequency table. Answer the questions.

Frequency of boys' names in Star School							
Matthew	John	Sandip	Callum	Wayne	Sean	Michael	Abdul
16	18	14	11	8	6	15	5

Which names are:

1 Most common?
2 Least common?
3 Second most common?
4 Second least common?

Discuss these questions with a partner:
- Your school might have different names. Why might this be?
- Will the most frequently used names be the same in all schools?
- Why might it make a difference where a school is?

Look around your classroom. Count the numbers of:

5

chairs

tables

drawers

windows

shelves

Draw a frequency chart to represent these.

Bar graphs

Study the bar graph. Answer the questions.

Survey of types of book read

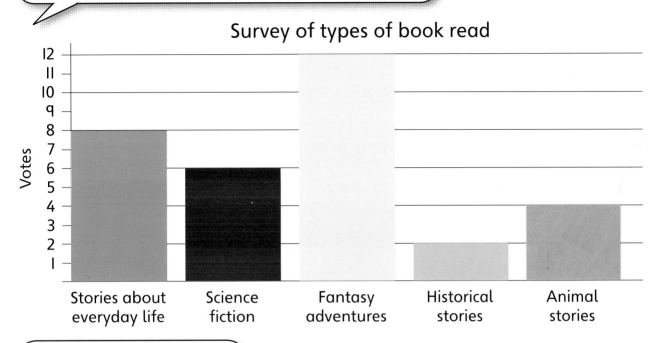

Which type of story is:

1   most popular?
2   least popular?
3   liked by 8 children?

How many children:

4   like the most popular story type?
5   like animal stories?
6   like animal stories or science fiction?

Work out how many children were asked if each child had just one vote. How about if each child had two votes?

Frequency tables

Study the frequency table. Answer the questions.

Favourite teams in Buzz School, Class 3 and Class 4						
Manchester United	Arsenal	Liverpool	Newcastle	Rangers	Chelsea	Cardiff
28	14	13	9	7	11	4

1 Which is the least popular team?

2 Which teams' votes total 20?

3 How many more votes has the most popular team got than the next most popular?

4 Which three teams have the same number of votes as Manchester United?

5 How many votes would Liverpool need to catch Manchester United?

6 How many votes would Cardiff need to catch Arsenal?

Why might favourite teams vary in different schools? List the six teams you would use for a survey in your school.

Bar graphs

Look at the bar graph. Answer the questions.

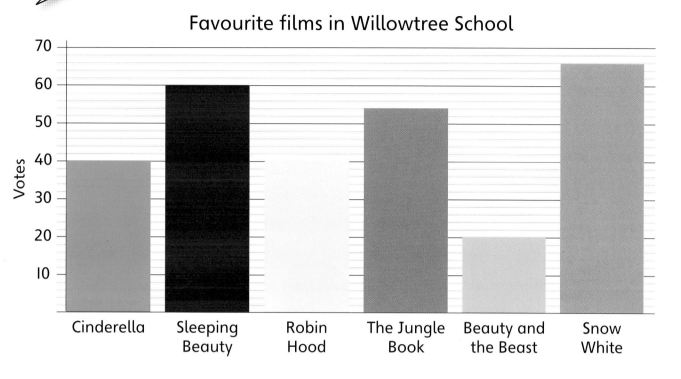

Favourite films in Willowtree School

1   Draw the frequency table from which this bar graph was drawn.

2   Which two films are liked by the same number of children?

3   Which film is the most popular?

4   Which film is the least popular?

5   How many children like Robin Hood?

6   How many more children like Sleeping Beauty than like Beauty and the Beast?

Carry out your own film survey, using your friends' opinions.

Bar graphs

Use a page from a reading book to collect data. Copy and complete the frequency table. Then draw the bar graph.

1

Survey of word length in my book						
1-letter words	2-letter words	3-letter words	4-letter words	5-letter words	6-letter words	More than 6 letters

2   What is the most common length of word?

3   What is the least common word length?

4   Which lengths of word occur the same number of times?

5   Is any length of word twice as common as another?

If you did the same survey for name length, how different would your findings be?

Adding and subtracting multiples of 10

Write the new heights.

I. $80 + 50 = 130 \, cm$

1 80 cm

grows 50 cm

2 63 cm

grows 40 cm

3  48 cm

grows 40 cm

4  92 cm

grows 80 cm

5 75 cm

grows 30 cm

6 56 cm

grows 50 cm

Copy and complete. Use a number grid to help.

7. $86 - 50 = 36$

41	42	43	44	45	46	47	48
51	52	53	54	55	56	57	58
61	62	63	64	65	66	67	68
71	72	73	74	75	76	77	78
81	82	83	84	85	86	87	88
91	92	93	94	95	96	97	98

7   $86 - 50 = \boxed{}$ 8 $75 - 20 = \boxed{}$

9   $92 - 30 = \boxed{}$ 10 $66 - 40 = \boxed{}$

11 $85 - 60 = \boxed{}$ 12 $71 - 50 = \boxed{}$

13 $36 - 10 = \boxed{}$ 14 $47 - 20 = \boxed{}$

15 $78 - 40 = \boxed{}$ 16 $55 - 40 = \boxed{}$

Use these cards 8 6 2 0 to make subtractions

like this $\boxed{}\,\boxed{} - \boxed{}\,\boxed{} = \boxed{}$.

How many answers can you find?

49

Adding and subtracting multiples of 10

Copy and complete.

1. 126 + 40 = 166

1 126 + 40 =

2 148 + 30 =

3 87 + 30 =

4 117 + 30 =

5 139 + 50 =

6 447 + 30 =

7 Ashok's guinea pig is too fat! It weighs 351 g. It loses 20 g. How much does it weigh now?

8 Gemma is walking to school. Her bag weighs 945 g. She returns a book to the library. She eats her apple and drinks her juice. How much does her bag weigh now?

9 Rob the rabbit is on a lettuce diet. He starts at 712 g. He loses 50 g each week. How much does he weigh after 5 weeks?

 Make up a word story for 496 g – 50 g.

Adding and subtracting multiples of 10

Write the new speed.

1. $446 + 50 = 496$ km/h

| 1 | 446 km/h | | 2 | 787 km/h | | 3 | 367 km/h | | 4 | 472 km/h |

1. 446 km/h — 50 km/h faster
2. 787 km/h — 50 km/h faster
3. 367 km/h — 30 km/h faster
4. 472 km/h — 40 km/h faster

5. 685 km/h — 50 km/h faster
6. 856 km/h — 60 km/h faster
7. 779 km/h — 40 km/h faster
8. 566 km/h — 60 km/h faster

Write the new heights.

9. $832 - 50 = 782$ m

9. 832 m — falls 50 m
10. 714 m — falls 60 m
11. 653 m — falls 60 m
12. 524 m — falls 70 m

13. 333 m — falls 60 m
14. 426 m — falls 40 m
15. 505 m — falls 50 m
16. 843 m — falls 60 m

A rocket starts at 500 m. It falls 40 m each second.
How many seconds until it touches down?
Make up a rocket landing problem for your friend to solve.

Adding and subtracting multiples of 10

Copy and complete.

1. $545 - 50 = 495$

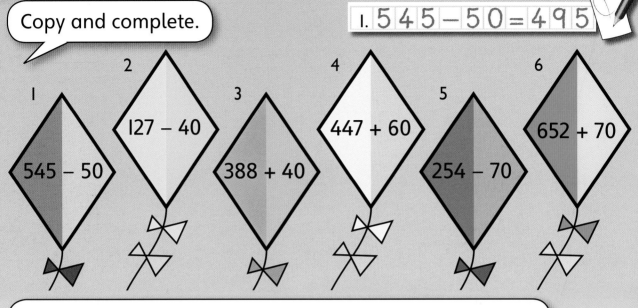

1. $545 - 50$
2. $127 - 40$
3. $388 + 40$
4. $447 + 60$
5. $254 - 70$
6. $652 + 70$

Add the money to the savings. How much is in each box?

7. $£1·48 + 70p = £2·18$

7. £1·48
8. £2·86
9. £4·64
10. £3·71
11. £1·59
12. £2·95

Kareena started with a score of 96. She got to 0 in 5 throws. What numbers could she have hit? What is the fewest throws she could have made?

13

10 20
5 4
1 3
50 2 30
40

Adding

> Use a number grid.
> Add the two numbers.

42	43	44	45	46	47	48	49	50
52	53	54	55	56	57	58	59	60
62	63	64	65	66	67	68	69	70
72	73	74	75	76	77	78	79	80
82	83	84	85	86	87	88	89	90
92	93	94	95	96	97	98	99	100

1. $64 + 21 = 85$

1	64 + 21	2	72 + 26
3	47 + 32	4	54 + 31
5	68 + 21	6	57 + 22
7	45 + 41	8	38 + 22

> How much to buy both comics?

9. $55p + 26p = 81p$

9

FLASH 55p   FUN 26p

10

Jack 63p   BOOM 27p

11

Sweet 48p   Puzzler 53p

12

WMF 39p   bike 42p

13

EPLOCK 56p   V 46p

14

CANDY 45p   PONY 28p

> Make up pairs of objects with prices which add up to £1.

Adding and subtracting

How much has each child got left after buying a ticket?

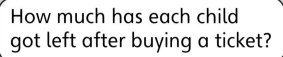
1. 8 5 p − 2 2 p = 6 3 p

1 22p
got 85p

2 22p
got 64p

3 15p
got 88p

4 34p
got 95p

5 33p
got 77p

6 23p
got 53p

Explore pairs of numbers with differences of 8, 18, 28… .

How much if the two drivers add their money together?

7. £4 6 + £2 5 = £7 1

7 £46 £25

8 £58 £135

9 £127 £45

10 £116 £56

11 £24 £39

12 £66 £55

Adding and subtracting

Write the new weight.

1. $328 + 48 = 376 \text{ g}$

1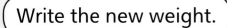
328 g
gains 48 g

2
454 g
gains 38 g

3
562 g
gains 39 g

4
434 g
gains 57 g

5
669 g
gains 28 g

6
375 g
gains 22 g

7

Take a 2-digit number and reverse the digits. 34 43
Take the smaller number from the
larger number. $43 - 34 = 9$
Repeat this. What do you notice?

How much further to go?

8. $374 - 23 = 351 \text{ km}$

8 374 km driven 23 km

9 278 km driven 42 km

10 165 km driven 33 km

11 585 km driven 44 km

12 294 km driven 52 km

13 245 km driven 34 km

Adding and subtracting

Work out the cost of each meal.

1. £2·76 + 18p = £2·94

1

£2·76   18p

2

£3·25   28p

3

£1·75   32p

4

£2·60   15p

5

£3·85   18p

6

£2·80   15p

7 You are the teacher! This is Sarah's homework. Check it, and correct any wrong answers. Give Sarah a mark out of 10.

Be the Teacher

a   148 − 26 = 122   b   84 − 53 = 32

c   92 − 43 = 49   d   254 − 42 = 221

e   87 − 38 = 59   f   566 − 51 = 515

g   839 − 27 = 812   h   74 − 35 = 31

i   82 − 19 = 63   j   65 − 18 = 57

Write four subtractions. Make two of them wrong. Give them to your friend to mark.

Adding and subtracting

Write the new depth.

1. 274 + 40 = 314 m

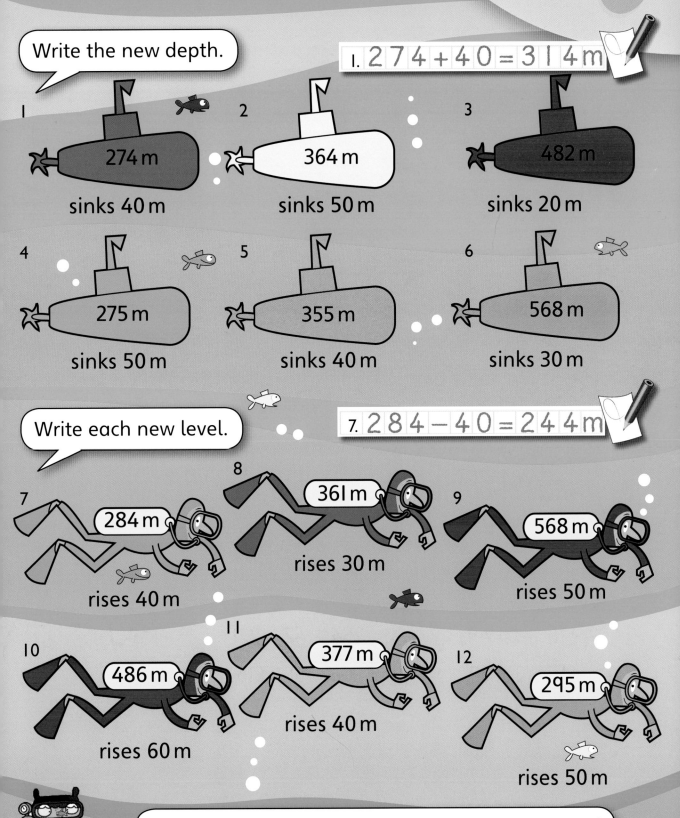

1. 274 m — sinks 40 m

2. 364 m — sinks 50 m

3. 482 m — sinks 20 m

4. 275 m — sinks 50 m

5. 355 m — sinks 40 m

6. 568 m — sinks 30 m

Write each new level.

7. 284 − 40 = 244 m

7. 284 m — rises 40 m

8. 361 m — rises 30 m

9. 568 m — rises 50 m

10. 486 m — rises 60 m

11. 377 m — rises 40 m

12. 295 m — rises 50 m

A diver rises 50 m and ends at between 200 m and 250 m. What depths could she have started at?

Adding and subtracting

Each child is reading a huge book! How many pages left to read?

1. $224 - 40 = 184$

1

I've read 40

224 pages

2

I've read 60

332 pages

3

I've read 30

512 pages

4 Jamie saves £20 each week. He starts with £176. How many weeks until he can buy a bicycle which costs £314?

5 Pooja has lived for 386 weeks. Her brother is 50 weeks younger than her. How old are they both? Remember: there are 52 weeks in a year.

Copy and complete.

6. $1400 + 300 = 1700$

6 1400 + 300

7 2500 + 400

8 3100 + 700

9 6200 + 400

10 1500 + 200

11 2200 + 700

12 4300 + 300

13 5500 + 400

14 3400 + 200

Work with a friend to write some additions like these where the total is a multiple of 1000.

$1400 + 600 =$

Adding and subtracting

Write each climber's new height.

1. $8400 - 300 = 8100\,m$

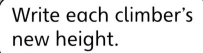

1 8400 m
climbs down 300 m

2 7800 m
climbs down 400 m

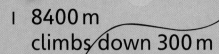

3 7500 m
climbs down 500 m

4 6900 m
climbs down 500 m

5 6400 m
climbs down 200 m

6 5800 m
climbs down 300 m

Each climber was sponsored to climb the mountain. Add the two cheques.

7. $£2700 + £500 = £3200$

7

£2700   £500

8

£4500   £600

9

£3600   £800

10
£5800   £500

I start at 1500 m. I climb down in multiples of 100 m, but I never climb down more than 400 m at any one time. How many ways of getting to the ground are there?

Adding and subtracting

How many adults in the crowd?

1. $2600 - 800 = 1800$

1 total: 2600
children: 800

2 total: 4100
children: 500

3 total: 5600
children: 900

4 total: 3300
children: 600

5 total: 1500
children: 700

6 total: 2400
children: 800

500 people were late. What is the total each time?

1. $2600 + 500 = 3100$

Copy and complete.

7. $23,800 + 500 = 24,300$

7 $23\,800 + 500$

8 $16\,200 + 800$

9 $38\,800 + 500$

10 $35\,700 + 700$

11 $14\,500 + 700$

12 $67\,400 + 800$

13 $26\,500 + 800$

14 $46\,800 + 800$

15 $54\,400 + 700$

My stadium holds 20 000 people. I can allow for up to 1000 empty seats. What are the sensible ways of splitting the seats, in multiples of 1000, for home and away supporters?

> Copy and complete.
> Use a number grid to help.

1. $49 + 6 = 55$

23	24	25	26	27	28	29
33	34	35	36	37	38	39
43	44	45	46	47	48	49
53	54	55	56	57	58	59
63	64	65	66	67	68	69
73	74	75	76	77	78	79
83	84	85	86	87	88	89

1 $49 + 6 = \boxed{}$ 2 $27 + 9 = \boxed{}$

3 $38 + 9 = \boxed{}$ 4 $65 + 9 = \boxed{}$

5 $73 + 9 = \boxed{}$ 6 $46 + 9 = \boxed{}$

> Now try these!

7 $27 + 11 = \boxed{}$ 8 $43 + 11 = \boxed{}$ 9 $28 + 11 = \boxed{}$

> Each price is reduced by 9p. Write the new prices.

10. $78p - 9p = 69p$

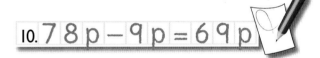

10 78p
11 65p
12 87p
13 56p
14 42p
15 64p
16 92p
17 85p
18 54p
19 43p

> Each price is reduced by 11p. Write the new prices.

> How many times can you take away 9 from 99?

Adding and subtracting

Copy and complete.

1. $224 + 29 = 253$

1 $224 + 29 = \boxed{}$

2 $342 + 19 = \boxed{}$

3 $148 + 29 = \boxed{}$

4 $563 + 21 = \boxed{}$

5 $236 + 19 = \boxed{}$

6 $472 + 21 = \boxed{}$

True or false?

7 To subtract 39, you take away 40, then take away 1 more.

8 To add 38, you add 40 then subtract 2.

9 31 less than a number is the same as 9 more than 40 less than a number.

How much is left after the ticket has been bought?

10. $£346 - £19 = £327$

10 £346
ticket: £19

11 £542
ticket: £19

12 £638
ticket: £19

13 £456
ticket: £21

14 £164
ticket: £21

15 £288
ticket: £31

Choose a 3-digit number with all the digits the same, e.g. 777. Add and subtract 19. Compare the units. What do you notice?

Adding and subtracting

Copy and complete.

1. $354 + 39 = 393$

1. $354 + 39 = \boxed{}$
2. $327 + 49 = \boxed{}$
3. $312 + 29 = \boxed{}$
4. $332 + 29 = \boxed{}$
5. $325 + 59 = \boxed{}$
6. $443 + 39 = \boxed{}$

7. Sid Seal is fed 250 tiny fish each day.

7. $250 - 29 = 221$

How many does he eat each day?

How many fish are not eaten altogether?

Monday	Leaves 29
Tuesday	Leaves 41
Wednesday	Leaves 99
Thursday	Leaves 19
Friday	Leaves 39
Saturday	Leaves 59
Sunday	Leaves 119

Write the new prices.

8. £$582 -$ £$39 =$ £543

8. £582
£39 off

9. £476
£29 off

10. £553
£31 off

11. £397
£51 off

How many times can you subtract 59 from 1000? Guess first!

Adding and subtracting

How many people on the ferry?

1. $475 + 49 = 524$

1   475 people
    49 get on

2   268 people
    49 get on

3   382 people
    41 get on

4   550 people
    59 get on

5   281 people
    69 get on

6   198 people
    59 get on

7   376 people
    51 get on

8   498 people
    41 get on

How many people on the aeroplane?

9. $512 - 49 = 463$

9   512 people
    49 get off

10 642 people
    59 get off

11 337 people
    41 get off

12 424 people
    51 get off

13 532 people
    49 get off

14 618 people
    39 get off

15 323 people
    41 get off

16 415 people
    59 get off

Write the last three digits of your telephone number. How many times must you add 4 to get to 1000? Try your friend's telephone number.

Fives and tens

Write a multiplication for each set of toes.

1. $3 \times 10 = 30$

1

2

3

4

5

6

7

 How many toes in your classroom? Include your teacher.

Write a multiplication for each set of fingers.

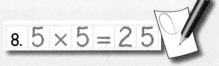
8. $5 \times 5 = 25$

8

9

10

11

12

13

14

15

16

Fives and tens

Write the value of each pile of coins.

1. $3 \times 5p = 15p$

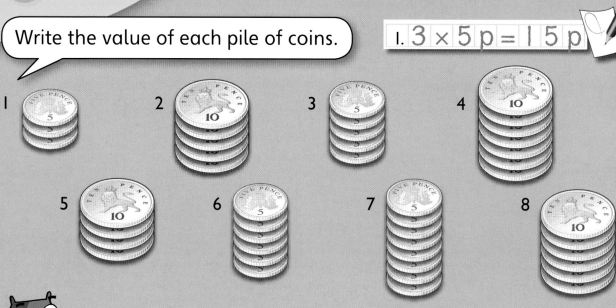

1   2   3   4

5   6   7   8

Write what must be added to make each pile worth £1.

Write the position of the pointer on each stick.

9. 15

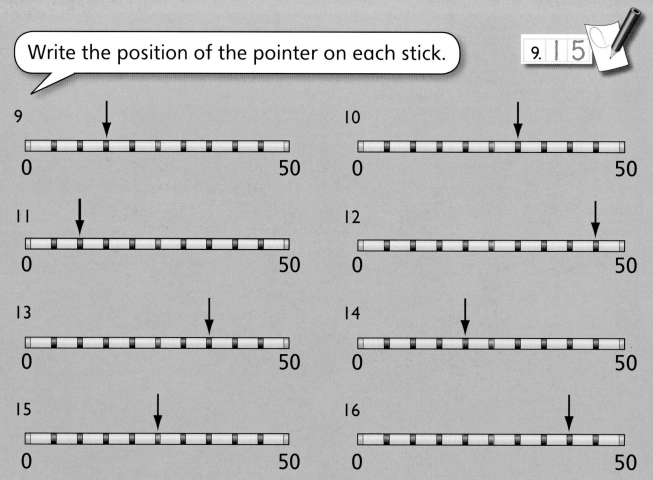

9   10
0   50   0   50

11   12
0   50   0   50

13   14
0   50   0   50

15   16
0   50   0   50

Fives and tens

Write the cost.

1. $4 \times 5p = 20p$

Soak the Teacher

5p a throw

l	4 throws	2	2 throws	3	7 throws
4	10 throws	5	20 throws	6	6 throws

Find how many throws you can have for each coin: lp, 2p, 5p, l0p, 50p, £1, £2...

Copy and complete.

7. $4 \times 5 = 20$

7 $4 \times 5 =$ 8 $6 \times 10 =$ 9 $7 \times 5 =$ 10 $4 \times 10 =$

11 $6 \times 5 =$ 12 $8 \times 5 =$ 13 $7 \times 10 =$ 14 $9 \times 10 =$

A trick for multiplying by 5 is:

multiply by 10, then halve it

For example: 9×5 ⟶ $9 \times 10 = 90$
half of $90 = 45$

Use the trick to try these:

15 $7 \times 5 =$ 16 $12 \times 5 =$ 17 $21 \times 5 =$

18 $32 \times 5 =$ 19 $46 \times 5 =$ 20 $14 \times 5 =$

Fives and tens

Copy and complete these divisions.

1. $35 \div 5 = 7$

1	$35 \div 5 =$	2 $80 \div 10 =$	3 $40 \div 5 =$
4	$60 \div 10 =$	5 $25 \div 5 =$	6 $70 \div 10 =$
7	$15 \div 5 =$	8 $40 \div 10 =$	9 $45 \div 5 =$

Write a matching multiplication for each.

10   Gill collects 5p coins in a jar. She collects 7 in the first week and 5 in the next week. How many coins does she now need to make £1?

11   45 players arrive for the school 5-a-side competition. How many teams can be made?

12   42 children are going by car on a school trip. Each car can take 5 children. How many cars are needed?

A trick for dividing by 5 is:

divide by 10, then double it

For example: $80 \div 5$ ⟶ $80 \div 10 = 8$
double $8 = 16$

Use the trick to try these:

13 $60 \div 5 =$	14 $90 \div 5 =$	15 $70 \div 5 =$
16 $160 \div 5 =$	17 $120 \div 5 =$	18 $230 \div 5 =$

Multiplying

Write pairs that show the same multiplication.

1. a and d

a

b

c

d

e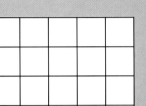

f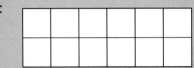

g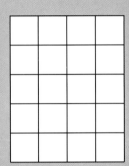

h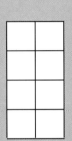

i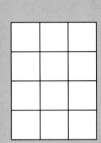

j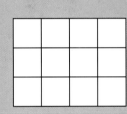

Use 12 squares to draw as many rectangles as you can.

Write the numbers in the reverse order and complete the multiplication.

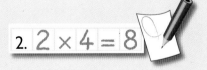
2. $2 \times 4 = 8$

2 4×2 3 3×5 4 8×2

5 4×6 6 7×3 7 2×9

8 6×3 9 5×4 10 6×7

Multiplying

Write two multiplications for each set of pegs.

1. $2 \times 4 = 8$
   $4 \times 2 = 8$

1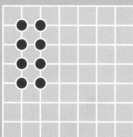

2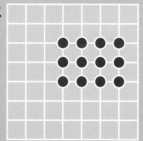

3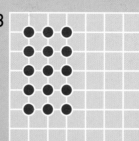

4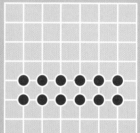

5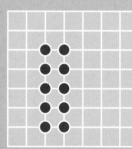

6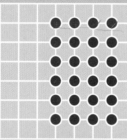

7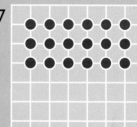

8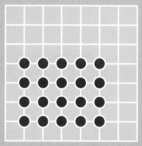

Copy and complete.

9 $3 \times 3 = \boxed{}$

10 $4 \times 2 = \boxed{}$

11 $5 \times 5 = \boxed{}$

12 $5 \times 2 = \boxed{}$

13 $3 \times 5 = \boxed{}$

14 $4 \times 3 = \boxed{}$

How many different multiplications can you show on a 6×6 pegboard? Use between 10 and 20 pegs.

Draw them on squared paper.

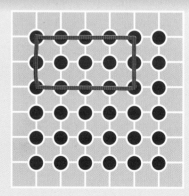

Multiplying and dividing

Write a division to match.

1. $12 \div 3 = 4$

1

2

3

4

5

6

Write two multiplications for each.

Copy and complete. Write two divisions to match each.

7   $3 \times 5 =$ ☐

8   $4 \times 6 =$ ☐

9   $5 \times 7 =$ ☐

10   $2 \times 8 =$ ☐

11   $6 \times 3 =$ ☐

12   $10 \times 4 =$ ☐

13   $8 \times 5 =$ ☐

14   $5 \times 4 =$ ☐

15   $9 \times 10 =$ ☐

Use these cards:
| 6 | 3 | 4 | 2 | 12 | = | ÷ | × |

Investigate how many different multiplications and divisions can be made.

| 12 | ÷ | 4 | = | 3 |

Multiplying and dividing

Copy and complete the multiplication table.

1

×	1	2	3	4	5	6
1						
2				8		
3						
4						
5						
6						

2 Choose five numbers in the table, and write two divisions for each.

2. $8 ÷ 4 = 2$
$8 ÷ 2 = 4$

True or false?

3 Two 5p coins have the same value as five 2p coins.

4 Five 10p coins have the same value as ten 5p coins.

Use the results to complete these:

$4 × 12 = 48$ $6 × 24 = 144$ $8 × 15 = 120$

$8 × 12 = 96$ $4 × 24 = 96$

5 $48 ÷ 4 = \boxed{}$ 6 $24 ÷ 6 = \boxed{}$ 7 $120 ÷ 8 = \boxed{}$

8 $96 ÷ 4 = \boxed{}$ 9 $96 ÷ 12 = \boxed{}$ 10 $120 ÷ 15 = \boxed{}$

11 $15 × 8 = \boxed{}$ 12 $24 × 4 = \boxed{}$ 13 $144 ÷ 6 = \boxed{}$

Threes

Frog starts at 0 and hops along the bank in 3s. Write a multiplication to show where he will be after:

1. $4 \times 3 = 12$

1. 4 jumps
2. 6 jumps
3. 3 jumps
4. 10 jumps
5. 8 jumps
6. 5 jumps
7. 9 jumps
8. 2 jumps
9. 7 jumps

How many jumps does Frog need to reach:

10. $9 \div 3 = 3$

10. 9
11. 15
12. 27
13. 6
14. 30
15. 21
16. 12
17. 24
18. 18

Frog starts at 0 and does one hop every minute. What number does he reach in an hour?

Threes and sixes

Each clover has three leaves. Write the number of leaves in each set.

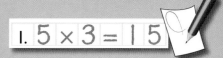

1. $5 \times 3 = 15$

1

2

3

4

5

6

Complete the rhyme up to 10×10.

$1 \times 3 = 3$, bee
$2 \times 3 = 6$, sticks
$3 \times 3 = 9$, line

Copy and complete 10 rows. Write the last number in the:

7. 12

1	2	3	4	5	6
7	8	9	10	11	

7 4th row   8 7th row

9 2nd row   10 10th row

11 5th row   12 6th row

Write the next 10 row ends in the pattern without drawing the table.

Threes and sixes

Copy and complete.

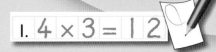
1. $4 \times 3 = 12$

1
4×3
4×6

2
5×3
5×6

3
8×3
8×6

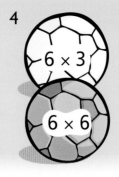
4
6×3
6×6

5
9×3
9×6

Write the position of the pointer on each stick.

6. 9

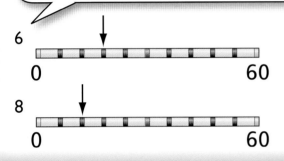
6

0   60

8

0   60

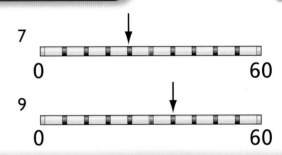
7

0   60

9

0   60

Football teams get 3 points for a win and 1 point for a draw. Write the number of points.

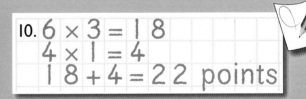
10. $6 \times 3 = 18$
$4 \times 1 = 4$
$18 + 4 = 22$ points

10 Arsenal
6 wins
4 draws

11 Chelsea
8 wins
3 draws

12 Manchester United
9 wins
5 draws

13 Liverpool
4 wins
6 draws

14 Newcastle United
7 wins
4 draws

15 Aston Villa
3 wins
2 draws

Find the points if teams get 4 points for a win and 2 points for a draw.

Threes and sixes

Copy and complete.

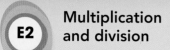

1. $6 \div 3 = 2$

1 $6 \div 3$
2 $15 \div 3$
3 $18 \div 6$
4 $24 \div 6$
5 $30 \div 6$
6 $21 \div 3$
7 $42 \div 6$
8 $18 \div 3$
9 $48 \div 6$
10 $27 \div 3$

11 Glen trains 3 times a week. How many weeks does it take to train 27 times?

12 How many teams of 3 can be made from a class of 25 children? How many left over?

Write the position of the pointer on each stick.

13. 150

13   0   300

14   0   600

15   0   600

16   0   300

Copy and complete.

17 4×60
18 6×30
19 3×30
20 9×60
21 5×60
22 7×30

Fractions

1. $\frac{1}{4}$

How many quarters are coloured?

1 　　2 　　3 　　4

How many fifths?

5 　　6 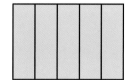　　7 　　8

How many eighths?

9 　　10 　　11 　　12

Write the coloured fraction.

13. $\frac{3}{4}$

13 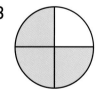　14 　15 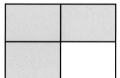　16 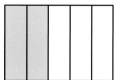　17

18 　19 　20 　21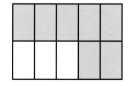

Work with a friend. Draw a rectangle to show $\frac{9}{10}$. Can you do one for $\frac{13}{25}$?

Fractions

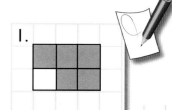

Copy each grid and colour the fraction.

1. $\frac{5}{6}$

2. $\frac{3}{4}$

3. $\frac{5}{8}$

4. $\frac{5}{9}$

5. $\frac{2}{5}$

6. $\frac{2}{3}$

7. $\frac{7}{10}$

8. $\frac{3}{6}$

9. $\frac{3}{8}$

Write the fraction of each grid that is not coloured.

1. $\frac{1}{6}$

 Work with a partner. Take turns to say a fraction, e.g. $\frac{5}{8}$. Your partner says the fraction to make a whole, e.g. $\frac{3}{8}$.

Write what fraction of the set is:

10. $\frac{4}{8}$

10 red

11 black

12 hearts

13 clubs

14 not diamonds

15 more than 5

16 less than 7

17 odd numbers

18 even numbers

Fractions

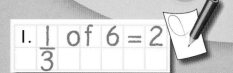
1. $\frac{1}{3}$ of 6 = 2

Write the number of buns.

1. $\frac{1}{3}$ of 6

2. $\frac{2}{3}$ of 6

3. $\frac{3}{3}$ of 6

4. $\frac{1}{4}$ of 12

5. $\frac{2}{4}$ of 12

6. $\frac{3}{4}$ of 12

7. $\frac{1}{5}$ of 20

8. $\frac{3}{5}$ of 20

9. $\frac{4}{5}$ of 20

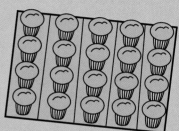

Copy and complete.

10. $\frac{3}{4}$ of 8

11. $\frac{2}{5}$ of 10

12. $\frac{7}{10}$ of 20

13. $\frac{3}{5}$ of 15

14. In a class of 30 children, $\frac{2}{3}$ are boys. How many girls are there?

15. The school team played 20 matches. They won one half of them and drew two-fifths. How many matches did they lose?

16. Raj bought a bag of 16 plums, but $\frac{5}{8}$ were bad. How many could he eat?

Write your own story for $\frac{3}{4}$ of 8 = 6.

Fractions

Copy and complete.

1. $\frac{2}{3}$ of $9 = 6$

1   $\frac{2}{3}$ of 9

2   $\frac{1}{3}$ of 6

3   $\frac{2}{7}$ of 21

4   $\frac{3}{8}$ of 16

5   $\frac{5}{6}$ of 12

6   $\frac{2}{3}$ of 12

7   $\frac{1}{7}$ of 14

8   $\frac{3}{8}$ of 24

9   $\frac{7}{8}$ of 16

Which is the greater?

10   $\frac{2}{3}$ of 9   or $\frac{1}{4}$ of 8

11   $\frac{3}{5}$ of 10   or $\frac{3}{4}$ of 12

12   $\frac{4}{7}$ of 14   or $\frac{5}{6}$ of 12

13   $\frac{7}{8}$ of 16   or $\frac{4}{5}$ of 20

14   $\frac{4}{10}$ of 50   or $\frac{5}{6}$ of 60

I can find $\frac{2}{3}$ and $\frac{3}{4}$ of 12. Help me find the other numbers you can do this for.